BELOVED
REVOLUTIONARY
SWEETHEART

BEATRIZ HAUSNER

BELO

REVOLUTIONA

BEATRIZ HAUSNER

OVED

RY SWEETHEART

Book*hug Press

Library and Archives Canada Cataloguing in Publication
Title: Beloved revolutionary sweetheart / Beatriz Hausner.
Names: Hausner, Beatriz, author.
Description: First edition.
Identifiers: Canadiana (print) 20200194194 | Canadiana (ebook) 20200194208
     ISBN 9781771665933 (softcover) | ISBN 9781771665940 (HTML)
     ISBN 9781771665957 (PDF) | ISBN 9781771665964 (Kindle)
Subjects: LCGFT: Poetry.
Classification: LCC PS8565.A79 B45 2020 | DDC C811/.6—dc23

PRINTED IN CANADA

The production of this book was made possible through the generous assistance of the Canada Council for the Arts and the Ontario Arts Council. Book*hug Press also acknowledges the support of the Government of Canada through the Canada Book Fund and the Government of Ontario through the Ontario Book Publishing Tax Credit and the Ontario Book Fund.

Book*hug Press acknowledges that the land on which we operate is the traditional territory of many nations, including the Mississaugas of the Credit, the Anishnabeg, the Chippewa, the Haudenosaunee and the Wendat peoples. We recognize the enduring presence of many diverse First Nations, Inuit and Métis peoples and are grateful for the opportunity to meet and work on this land.

Book*hug Press

I love you more than Seguin did Valence,
And how I'd like to conquer you in love,
My dearest friend, for you're by far the greatest
—The Countess of Dia, often called Beatritz

CONTENTS

THE IMPORTANCE OF HUMAN ROMANCE

THE ORGASM ELEGIES

NOTES

TIED

UP

High Priestess

Our revered lords ladies dear ones I am come to render elegant
homage to silks sometimes chains due to the reversal of the bias.

The principal altar is up side down. Divine Adoratrice of Amun
you of the easy knit interacting with the holder of the office, use

yourself as inspiration in moiré and the shimmery legs strutting
down the aisle: May the perfect fabrications reach up to you because

nothing detracts from the treatment the modality of those fabrics
draped against hardware. You command our attention to the mirror

of ourselves your subjects. Because you must on your own place
the ethereal layers and it is necessary to conceal your love of these

the mothers of the children hanging off us women who accept
the wearing of garments for our Lord Love of perfect fit. Around

us rise the hanging gardens of Babylon and Alexander who saw
them and mistakenly fled along the grain yes against the grain for

he knew not the power of adjuration entreaty renewed twice yearly
when we sat along the long path and praised the importance of the

collar to Amun God's Wife you are God's Wife of Amun they call
you more than all the vestals at the altar you alleviate suffering and

the sisters moan in a blessed tone as the trombone groans with the
seasons of irreverence are we renewed spring summer fall and

winter the collections are with the art of being from which we animate
ourselves. I entreat you: do nothing don't do anything to your genders

of sex for him not the fulfillment of desire nor the satisfying
of want though getting to coming requires great creative power

and the constant invention of writing where pleasure is a present
couture placed against ready-to-wear for the young ones who

work seamlessly and in heels. The young secretariat records
your dictum: I belong to a world devoted to elegance. The

manner of your prayer makes us the thing that most suits you
from which flows our cosmology and structure and softness and

masculine and feminine sometimes the unflattering silhouettes
of ugly chic luxury albeit not basted but rather shirred so

that normalizing the unexplored when designing on paper
when fabricating when draping when cutting when sewing

when finishing the fabric is the medium. Pre-eminently
wearable with the figure dictating the shape of those garments

you offer your chest of accessories drawers that open
and close of their own will overflowing fruit crushed

in a glass of blue of green jewels inside alcohol. We
travel in a car pulled by two lapdogs whose names are

princely.

A designer also this Theodora your sister of now utilizing
whole with no exterior construction to force the dress into

place—and you must be patient. You must surpass yourself
to reach your goals—you utter as the flame is lit and you close

your eyes in prayer pull the flame to your cheeks with your
hands and kiss the deities invisibly protecting us warrior

women in file we parade before you, we who are
fierce and strong, impenetrable owners of our sex.

Song on Tongue

When least expected
        you arrive with
                song on your tongue
                        revenant king

nestled with our sexes

present yourself
        that I might see you
                shackled to strange
                        furniture

love hidden

by the textures of want
        I travel the length
                of your body with my lips

I touch

your geographic markers
        west to east
                movement
                        stasis

always the heart

let us not bury
        the distressed moan
                not place the slab
                        over us

nor live
        with exculpation
                in dream

a star rises to your lips
        to your hair made
                of filaments of gold
                        and of fabulous

smoke
        with Moro anchoring
                this voice you enter
                        the room and tap
                                lightly on nerves

that grow inward from my sex
        now caught in the jaws
                of the lion

let us meet daily and at
        the hour proscribed
                by sun clocks

        exact premonitions

of surrender
      let us
             love to excess before
                  someone invisibly turns
                       the hue of my skin to indigo

before they place a bowl of blood
      in one hand lotus flower
      in the other
          a snake
               in my third hand

and I am not done:

I place one foot on your chest
      another foot on your sex
          and I dream you awake

you who must be mine
      if I am to vanquish the armies
          that make war inside the man
             and the woman that we are despite

ourselves

So soon as the front of you

So soon as the front of you is noticed
you become obscured

                    sweet apple turn

to stone the darkness

                  within

as the purl hot
no-not cold
swirls again yes
and interminably
within you
without you

                because who would not take

sadness with your ecstasy?

Together we pour ourselves
out and into me with

                your great swelling

your soul inherited
and further burnished
through strange marriages
with darkness:
the union is almost
complete in obscurity
as someone else's hands
close your doors.

Do not take these breasts
into belly not and yes

          below your chest laid bare

I see your heart open wound
weeping song of remembrance
released before the ages multiply
and

         ah how slender

the trunk of the tree holding
up the weight of your night
and your fear of loss
and my constant releasing
of you to yourself and to darkness

inherited from the mothers
who roped tightly into knots

        your hips

such attraction turned
your thighs underneath
away from white
ice sheets and black snow
and the cutting knife baring
the song of weeping

                the very image of shapeliness

is too slow indeed
in hiding though
indeed unfortunately
I am not able

                to bear it witness

for you are inward gone
not deep inward but
somewhat inbound
this inwardness without
you and I am not able

        to bear to bear to bear to bear to bear it.

Tied Up

Speech and knife cut through sense making
as time slips in and out of us first and last
and original sun radiating from among the
myriad stars that

explode in the night blackest of darkness where
your forebears lived with strange creatures as you
began your confinement

in and out

of forms with the Countess of Dia
sometimes called Beatritz.

—The animals of my country—you say.

Please tell me why my car is in the front yard
And I'm sleeping with my clothes on. I came in
through the window last night and you're gone

you write as you attach to the ghost of Jaufre
Rudel with those voices now ours spoken
through strange machines that come to our
rescue for we live together with our sexes

first wealth of joy.

You inscribe your path on the course of my
night my day on my back. Present yourself
so I may see you shackled to strange furniture
where love remains hidden in fabric's folds.

I who am relentlessly drawn to these outward signs of inward
subversion because of want will travel the length of
your body with my lips touch your geographic
markers finally become cruel inside the body suit

I ideate bondage

of man of woman bringing us closer
to the lifestyles of strange insects.

—I could put one of those on—I remember saying
and let me point out that the outfit made of shimmering
rhinestones and metal mesh is laid out and ready yes

such is the manner of my being beautiful for
you disguised sharply with my edges under gold
and silver thread turning myself more appropriately
into the praying mantis you so often marry.

In night and in the light of day over there for some
hope of help but later it comes back and tells me it would
be hard to slip away because I can trace your singing

I who am your mistress become lighter as I dress
myself in the manlike suit made from ethereal layers
of fabric the better to expose my soul to fishnet
and may my skin not show.

My completeness is breathlessly held up
by the tiresome suspension of time you
subject me to. Barely audibly and despite
the bindings

I get on top.

Movement and stasis and
giving it and taking it.

Let's stop this being in the heart's chambers
try it without love and openly before the secret
overwhelms itself and consumes us in flames.

Missed pleasure surrender
in darkness and in light
alternating states shimmery
veils that move with the rain.

Distress of the heart that lives outside covered
in the matter of liquid skin that is warm and bright
and not dark nor intense.

I am your reverent:

I praise not the transience of your sex
once carried with briefness from East back
to West of the great river you must travel
now laterally with your sidelong glance
become glint become black stone bear it
on your back until your tenderness
is mine and is yielding. We herald
togetherness for ourselves even and

we are driven on beset by our temptations and our trials.

Question: Where is he placed?
Answer: Within six walls.

Question: Where is it?
Answer: Up down before behind right left.

Someone is stitching you to me.
An assured hand drives the needle
and its shimmery thread. Pull me
to you that I may hasten my pleasure
and not be brave.

Last question: What is man like?
Answer: An apple.

Because I Am Beatrice

Amor tenendo / meo core in mano...
... Poi la svegliava, e d'esto core ardendo
                                        —Dante

I will not relinquish
Your heart in my mouth

I will swallow the words written on
Your heart in my mouth

I will take away sorrow as long as I have
Your heart in my mouth

I will walk a great distance to reach
Your heart in my mouth

I will stop walking a great distance to reach
Your heart in my mouth

I never want to stop coming to being with
Your heart in my mouth

I grow increasingly impatient if I don't have
Your heart in my mouth

I ignore the fact of new discoveries in astronomy because I have
Your heart in my mouth

Stars are born die and are reborn in the veins that feed
Your heart in my mouth

There is a great ocean we must cross as we voyage into
Your heart in my mouth

And what a deafening joy as music fills my throat because I have
Your heart in my mouth

I speak only to you when I have
Your heart in my mouth

The sun the moon at midday the eclipse with
Your heart in my mouth

We step out of ourselves are in thrall as stars explode with
Your heart in my mouth

So many times there comes into my mind the ideation of being with
Your heart in my mouth

There are no limits to what I can do with
Your heart in my mouth

Several constellations are born when I have
Your heart in my mouth

Liquid skin is the element that constitutes
Your heart in my mouth

I don't care about the quotidian if I have
Your heart in my mouth

Flocks of nightingales become airborne with
Your heart in my mouth

Says Aristotle the soul sits in the heart and this supports the fact of
Your heart in my mouth

A life-size tiger breathing and preponderant threatens to appropriate
Your heart in my mouth

Great dangers precede and follow my single-most objective:
Your heart in my mouth

I have determined to rewrite the treatise on alchemy to explain
Your heart in my mouth

Determined also that gold is a liquid poured from a great flask
    suspended above
Your heart in my mouth

Innate always is the state of love because I persist in holding
Your heart in my mouth

The body, the soul and the spirit, they have become one with
Your heart in my mouth

THEOD
BIBLIO

DORAE

OTECA

The Dream of Theodora

I. Theodora Inchoate

Inchoate and first inside the shapes of mountains and their soft edges
promulgations of forms their precipitous sharpness already inside her

always with gentle voice of father and of mother who loved her
and would constantly though the ghosts were not soothing for

they announced overwhelming illuminations in darkness. Even so
the mountains persisted topped by light and constant promise of

the beyond with snows announcing another Other and same with big
people and their tenebrous inheritance of pain forcing memorization

and torment of memory of the cruellest cipher: 71594. Enumerations
etched by efficiency generated by early algorithms tattooed for the ages

by the devastation machine. Such was demonic catastrophe always
    ghostly
rubbing against the new life of parents who kept on being and non-
    being in

crepuscular states inside and outside the ash the bounden reverence
to fear in the chambers as the gas was inhaled for generations to come.

Gloom.
     Dance.
         Gloom.

Despite the dialectic felicity lived there as conveyance of joy descended
from fortunate wandering exiles they survived conditionally nestled in
     valleys
         alive
            thankfully
               living.

II. Theodora Incipient

The Andes, reminder of the littleness of childhood fragility because
spring runoff is eternal and downward pulled by cheerful gravity

doing what gravity does with plate tectonics interrupting the more
gentle movements of the earth. All being upended with irregular

frequency the shards of glass lined the floor of the loved childhood
home. The first kingdom was a place long and narrow with obstruct-

ions of view defining geography on the road to Theodora. Paradise
was always the goal. John of Ephesus described it. All that matters

is of Ephesus born. Ephesus of the mind, because the goddess is revered
there despite the excessive number of breasts crowding her

chest. Ephesus is Chile. An open-and-shut case. A country with its St.
Jamestown at centre Serenetown at north Conceptiontown middling

south and Sandpoint town closest to antipodal Antarctic with the
Southern Cross replicating the Morning Star illuminating all the things

that were one at origin: Light.

III. Theodora Forming

Source. Let's speak in terms of The Secret History for all histories are
secret like the rooms where she lay as a child listening to the sounds

of the wounded animal her father rescued from a hole and carried
to safety in his arms as he came down the mountain. Different beings.

Tenderness they were and not made of flesh and blood. Standing on its
hinds the bear roared as Theodora grew hoarse within her tiny bones

expanding the sinews in her throat voice muscularity of voice to serve
divine service of the heart through her other parts the ones still coming

together and being made by invisible hands drawing patterns of sounds
winged birds for arms hers and legs hers. Pliability was always the

crux of the matter there where the rhythms of letters followed one
another and formed speedily and deeply attending effectuating

functioning pushing sound up the walls of her mouth as she slipped on
the ribbons of silken flesh waiting always elastic with patience the blow

came down cutting through her fear until the contortionist
was formed, readying the recreation of Theodora true. With her

father's beasts did she begin performing the shrill song moving toes
up the legs of the men who lascivious fell at her feet walked unwalked

the hours minute-counting the seconds inside the day
    until now.
Merging we become one Theodora. Byzantium is here constancy

shifting as bodies flow one into the other. Becoming flexible
we curve under pressure and do not break.

IV. Domina

Theodora they call me Theodora is my name edged on the tips
of these fingers by the little ants entering and exiting the book

of anguish Theodora I am as I enter the sacred precinct appraise
space assess guests multicoloured because they live with Isis whose

name means throne. I speak of ants again because fashioned from gold
and real fur though not prickly they pull away from the focus of my

parentage I who am daughter of Geb and wife of Sky-Heaven remove
my jewels. Tingling pendants come off my forehead as do the stacks

of bangles holding these forearms paying tribute always to the heiress
of gold of gems that are solid liquid glittering noiselessly like powder

covering skin under light. I ready myself for the performance.
Shadowed lids the sequined eyes are made visible the horizontal

slats collapse one into the other like the walls of a strange void.
Entering the temporary underworld daily I force myself to sleep-see

the awaited processional of my gods anteceded by strange birds that
glow with scales like iridescent fish despite the dryness of this place.

Hues of nacre dispel the absoluteness of darkness and for good.
Resolving to be alive I remove the last of these garments but for

a ribbon of silk cover the heart between these legs the better to conceal
the strange murmurs that mark time drawn by the assured hand of love.

I sink down and see myself as myself though I am myself third person
singular I remain and I sink further into and on the stage floor I arch

my back extremely. There are servants to whom it is entrusted the
scattering of the grains of barley from above into a calyx the passion

flower my sex where geese trained for the purpose next begin to pick
at the kernels one by one with their bills and eat. I rise a little feel the

stairs wrap themselves around my legs the mesh of stockings
their constriction. A slight tremor is felt as I surrender to the soft

and feathered surface my back.

Justinian's Dream

I. His Emergence

From her Antipodes emerged flesh and voice of ideal man her own
Dionysus nestled between ocean and mountains beyond where the

mother of his mother was at origin always outside even in hiding
the hymns were intoned and he could hear her voice through the

walls of her womb water sounding life. With and through writing
himself on this skin he is daily born. His was a mother related

in state to a queen named Calafia later incarnation of Semele
preceded out of chronology for they were referents women

who lived in fear and in anger and were apt to hide in trees
as they made their laboured crossing of the desert and filled

the land with promise. I remember the black sands—she would
say. Califerne was called the country of myth replications of Greece.

Father and mother gave joy as they created their ancestors and truth.
Source of life source of memory from life. From earliest devotion

prayer repeated Calafia was an Island of Amazons celebrated
by Rodríguez de Montalvo even, Don Quixote previously and

after because there was The Song of Roland before. I repeat they hailed
from Califerne. In his boy's games he delved into morning cartoons

the show's about to start! a moose large and a squirrel sidekick small.
Parallel figments separated by the ages. First was the marmot teasing

old Herodotus into believing they were ants throwing him into
confusion because of their being vastly numerous turning the hills

into pulsating skin the grass. Justinian as child his eyes saw
them (because I asked him and he said he did and still sees them;

outside is inside despite the fires that rage in his veins). Slowly
began forming the great handsomeness he carries about:

His-Appearance-Is-Brightness. He hides inside tomes written
and rewritten, his. New language of twined words upending

English even as he carries them around, beach reading same covers
alternating green red he intones one of the two Elvises Chapter Two:

I think I fell in love with you. Long and not so long ago and into
another time where want lives in the folds of time and the space

between is the threshold where we are sex that is heart becoming
and bestowing one to the other. Sex understood sex misunderstood.

Califerne not precisely California dreamin' but his mind finding itself
in Hesiod's Birth of the Divine Venus Philommedes, Cock-Swallower

at times Aphrodite he says as he goes about transforming things and
writing about the occult manner of Sky-Heaven's rejoicing when

conjuring vast Earth he hears her groan within as he spreads
himself full upon her entirely and with all the things that are

in nature. The gods are assembling before him as he writes them
and all around him as he excitingly begins giving form to the Divine

Theodora (his words) predicting her various permutations as he closes
his eyes and sees her tininess before the towering Andes her backdrop.

Youth arrives. Begins his interest in prosody. The mountains before him
though not so much because the sea is in front. Begins the science

learning of the Californian Tacitus his reasons for seeing persistent
mistranslations mistaken understandings of victories as failures.

Always questioning he collates the sources and appends the record.

II. The Lonely Wilds

He once bartered with replications of women who did battle
with animals large and small repeating alternate versions of

his mother the goddess that haunts rivers and lonely wilds proud
bearer of the name that stands for all outsiders variously distant.

There were animals large and small: the marmot, first tantalizer of
Herodotus (again). He was dazzled by the unnamed things of nature

misunderstanding insects translated poorly as creepers by questionable
sources whose eyes see double. There was the height of a Greek El

Dorado in the Himalayas. Surely the Rockies in reverse. Upside is
downside and regardless we return to our origins at his mother who

recalled the menacing black desert hills the canyons and the inland sea
where his ancestors built the temple among hymns and pledges. She

wrapped herself in denial of magic and wept silently into his infant
mouth as it searched for nourishment blood and bone sensing future

mirth. Abnegation came followed by postponement. He began
to think they all came from the Levant.

III. Every Day He Writes the Book

Every day he writes the book my Lord Aymar. Chapter One—this
morning's Ovidius Naso an accident come to hand—says he

and truth to tell my Lord Aymar is generous, gay and ostentatious
and knows not how to break free of the ties that bind him.

Downward. Silk restraints disguised as long sequences of vowels
and consonants rather when he is righteous courteous and pleasant so

is he the worthiest and he loses not his sense because rational in ways
familiar to the list makers who moan in despair as they bind him sew

him to the continuous spine he is haughty fierce and proud because
he is a good knight in the pages unbound all-seeing of the book he

writes entrenched or trenched wandering inside patterns of other
knights who would put valour and worth at stake solely because he is

not used to them nor was he then. He persists this knight he writes
the book every day erudition's ties pulling tightly at his words

—Dame Biatriz, your beautiful kindly countenance and the great beauty
and precious worth which are in you makes my art easily defeat the best

for it is gilded by your high and true merit— tradition of erotic
mysticism exchanging souls he goes on writing merging us into

a single body he goes on quoting Chaucerian riddles he cuts
and sews and binds their bodies renders their hearts permeable

sheer enjoyable pleasure of sex the deity's own considerate
invention he says embarking on Chapter Two out of pitch dark

he must exit the other life his lest his hands find other strange hands.

IV. Kali Cali Throughout

California knows how to party for a truth and zipping shaking together
shaking stepping lightly heavily shaking wildly the spots of the cat

around her hips collapse shake it shake it shake it shake it Cali keep on
stepping dancing lightly feet red blood on cock his her feet stepping

stepping lightly arms multiplying becoming circles transforming
visions of skulls into beings become free Cali shake it shake it shake it

jamming accelerating not slowing the party all over the temple
becoming long dance trance becoming tongue becoming voice

become coming in trance his cock swallowed constantly moving
away from his supine manner no longer Kali with him beneath

Kali facing face his becoming eye to eye lips to lips open mouth
to mouth shifting now positioning sexes that are mouth to sex

mouth to tongue mouth of voice in mouth in sex mouth with eye
in mouth trance image transmutation of being Cali-forni-a love

of sex Kali-for-nian love of sun destruction construction of love
is Kali Cali lives with sun-drenched pelt of leopard before her his

sex in voice her sex in his voice his voice in her sex Kali who
is turning forming shaping: Cali Cali Cali Cali Yeah that's right

West coast west coast Uh California love California love.

ISIS UP IN

THE AIR

Every Door Has Two Fronts

I.

every door has two fronts, this way and that

grown up yet a child you having it not having it taking it
taking it not taking it completely engaging on your knees

serving the deities replicating tongue on sex you having
it finally as the days turn hard come and say the new year

begins it is the cold season no longer the dream is cast
into visions renewed the muse was not then is now because

there is paucity in forward-moving repeated turnabout as
replications of house are lit from within your rooms are mine

notwithstanding the metrics are or are not sorrow alternating
joy as you pull me toward you by the throat stockings for bindings

facing you or from behind your cock is my acceptation sometimes
I say while you go on drawing patterns structures long ago discarded

by me who begins living daily as you tighten the noose holding me to
you no matter the changing colours fingernails dig into hands turn

them liquid as the ceremonials begin proceed so you may stop
substituting alternates for surrogates devising replacing ourselves

we go the mechanics are implied the tongue grows deep roots inside
outside the throat tingles stars explode in the night retract in day

every door has two fronts, this way and that

II.

absence presence of hands
around sound the veins hum
inside the mouth is held pleasure
tightly not released but coming
and getting to coming extremities
of want singling out one-at-a-time

entirely you
are in
handsomeness
you become
completely

despite your darkness perceived
when the windows are shuttered
of your own light remain still
own your light it flows out
of your sex affirmation pleasure

is a continuum
it is coiling and
linking the long
chain evolving
into voice born

deep within and since abolish
doubt negate destruction in ritual
and pose the question: where is
pleasure? answer: it lives with
the morning star in a crystal vessel

question:
who spoke it first?
answer:
César Moro

question: can want be understood?
answer: yes when voice gets
caught between two doors

repeat the question:
can want be understood?
there is no answer
last question: who spoke best?
answer: Ovid

on we go with our praying
as inside and outside become
animated with beings drawn
on the terracotta surfaces
when the Great Vates perhaps
the Countess of Dia or maybe
one not known sings the
black-on-ochre forms out
loud and proclaims

luckily, I take great joy of love

III.

here is my avidness repeating itself long since

    on tongue

at ends of fingers that draw images on clay
vessels that pour the liquid the exaggerated
inversions of their thighs are all that remains
of the men who were warriors battling against
their ghosts

            whatever lingua
            whenever tongue
            yes tongue again

tongue always enclosed by lips around
sounds that multiply between his legs now
between these inside is outside

            every door has two fronts
            this way and that

repeating on this day the tongue grows
deeper roots into itself to announce a
happy morning dawning inside her
vida changing measurably the days shaped

by lording love the shimmering fabrics
glisten and tremble in stranger spaces
braided ropes of metallic cotton chain the
lovers together into one is sewn tight the
weave so the ills they have and the lightness
build the garment we share

        impossible
        is possible

so let's undress these two bodies friend if
you had just one fourth of this aching that afflicts
me now as the throat constricts around pleasure
with sound nearing lips marking the
lettered words that call out for you to see

        back and front
        of time ends
        begins anew

every door has two fronts this way
and that the fires are lit they
are brightening the snow on
days marked by a hand unseen by
you who animate

        every door has two fronts
        this way and that

again let's say there is fire in the middle
of the lion's breast glistens the constellation
it flows out of horizontal nightfall and the fur
of the large cat lines the ancient walls of
temples enamelled on worn clay surfaces

       they tell the story
       of cock ingeminate

its esurience repeating images in yellow
ochre on black the warriors always with
so many intervening body parts becoming
appropriate because men drew them
not women who spoke without sound

       their famished
       voices being in
       want even

silence overwhelmed speech
joining intoning seek pleasure desire
rouse the tongue from sleep awaken to
pleasance to delight and come

       every door has two fronts
       this way and that

The Delightful Love Of Bacchus

Ariadne comes Bacchus comes this is whom the nymph
beheld despite the white mantle draped over darkness
destroy not my canes the growth of my streams the black
core inside the breathing of the world yet to be poured
from a single cup despite the disbelievers and their babble

juxtaposing now crossing over to the Bard say:
be not afeard; the isle is full of noises
Caliban explaining things maybe it happens

they are sounds and sweet airs, that give delight
and hurt not and come from deep waters
making skin sing inside crowding sounds
the animals those images the pigments
come alive ride on their backs and under them

and interfere with the bindings and noises are with their
mechanical contraptions becoming legged playthings they
are given help though there is the matter of their vociferations

less an imposition than interference in the making
of a perfect space where we might live with the
colours of these toenails ornaments for ideal feet
become sudden animals dead alive on our sides
as the linens billow out of control the beasts

that play inside an overflowing bowl held up by means
of our teeth and all manner of life is poured over our
ecstatic embrace brightness is made and despite the
darkness of the ancient devices let us say

> the god is now come and the fields resound
> with the wild cries of revellers

A Story of Egypt, Twisted

The goddess changes form often and usefully. She grinds her teeth she
curses and blesses whenever the enemies come between the love of
Osiris and Isis. Egypt is on tip of tongue and at nerve endings.

—All I want now is to boil the Hell out of myself—It's likely due to the
chatter I say, because it obscures the Blessed Queen of Heaven Ceres.
—Go to the sea and purify yourself—you say, as my various parts burn

one by one. Did I say that Isis always intervenes? Yes I may have said as
much because only she knows how to piece together the cut-up parts of
Osiris. Questing she goes up the Nile searching for the pieces

of her husband's body. She speaks oh but do let the elastic water
explore me as the vipers rise from left hand from right hand look at
the round disc forming itself on my brow and despite the consuming

light filtering itself down to you I appropriate the tissues that are to
make you complete. Restoring your cock I go. Not in the usual ways of
the sea and its sinking animals the ones that swim with the voracious

fishes that consumed it before was laid the mantle of dark so the stars
in your eyes would shine brightest Osiris I invoke you. Much after the
perfumes of Arabia were spent and the flowing waters turned

into rivers of sand, Gwendolyn, you said—At Mecca there is a sacred
well called the Zem Zem— I say come along explore me so you may find
your Egypt reconfigured returned to your dream of water here.

May the Goddess once again exculpate us from our too frequent falls
into the darkness of the north season. On the shores
of these waters we celebrate you our first priestess.

Isis Up in the Air

the brood of birds that
        we birthed three times
ten ages ago begin
        their slaughter as you set
yourself against yourself and
        lean on writing

        mostly

that is why the white dove, torn
from her mate, is often burned
upon Idalian hearths

the inverted is real
        you repeat yourself

in useless trips east of the Indus
        contrary
        to the movements
        of ancient heroes

reversal of being in the sadness of
those who unwalk the running game
as you go contesting Egyptian Isis.

She is identified with
Argive Io
usually
until recently

always reminding us of her power
goddess of the Nile echoing around us
who prevail making ours your parts

      dismemberment
              yours
                   was

I go on piecing you back together
with my feet firmly planted in this mud
I cry in the night as I rise in the winged
machine that elevates me to a city we
might one day live in because of the
ancient rituals practised there

the sacred books announce
a past of bloodletting and also
of peace arranged neatly by
the hand of the

Invisible One

may their powers
      not revoke
      not countermand
      not repeal
      not overturn
      not turn back
      not turn around
      nor change by reversal
      is my prayer

For Good and Ever

Where is the point of placement of the heart
and now by heaven?—you asked.

It is bleak hereabouts—was my answer. We both
prayed inside a house where the incantations

were shouted through devices placed inside the ear
and went mad with the din. The shrieking

animals never slept. Gone strange they were inside us
as we hunted them down. We went looking

for the goddess of misplaced likeness ours flailing limbs
knocking at the walls of our room away we

journeyed too much through distant being we became
source of water where happiness and giggling

reverberated in divinity. Now is the glimmering of liquids
our little people still drink they are small beings our

selves as when we met precious because of persistent
adoration our mutual fuzziness and the lasting

fondness between our legs where the rippling heat endures.
Abiding we go invoking our inheritance handed down

by the ancestors wanderers in the desert and still calling
us to live forwardly and retroactively for good and ever.

Thus we meet and daily at the lunate crossroads where
you my Moon-man and I Adoratrice of your Sun still

wander The-Levant-Of-The-Mind where we lie under a
blanket made of threads spun from mistlike purple flax.

Begins the Bright Season

heal this wound start to rest easy in your company
turn around make your case for the importance of human

romance between these legs you and your veins where
flows the liquid spice welling at your sex as the tie is

wrapped around your wrist in order to be joyous again
indeed—blood and fear and reticence hardened once

when silence echoed. Repent the mournful sounds.
Stop. Between your eyes is my heart. See this, we

stand at the beginning of the bright season indeed and
remember the black herons were perched on black rock

they cackled their song. Let me be the expert of your
ecstasy and repeat make your case for the importance

of human romance you who are kingly come indeed do
lie here and let us be you and I here as we stand at the

beginning of the new day we will dance among
us and with ourselves dance dance dance

THE IMPOR

HUMAN RO

TANCE OF

OMANCE

The Importance of Human Romance

I walk into an empty room
And suddenly my heart goes boom
—Eurythmics

I

I surrender and enter a great flame
blazing in my room like a burning
heart making all else disappear

> hold in your hand the thing
> completely all made of fire
> and speak to me:

tuus sum: I am yours.

> hold my figure in your arms
> surround me with that
> crimson cloth all over

such is my idolatry of you
the joy carried in my blood turning
these veins into knots of heat

> again hold in your hand the thing
> completely made of flame and
> speak to me: vide cor tuum

my heart I keep inside you
even as I burn I relinquish
my powers and may you consume
us and be absorbed in nuptial fire

> mine is cast in flames.
> I sleep and don't wake up

tuus sum: I am yours

my new life is reverie

II

the angel is standing
watch at the door

>do you feel his breathing
>as he now lies between us?

perhaps when you allow your
animals to be soft felines lightly
stepping on our bodies. Recall
too the languid afternoons
when heat was quieted sound
and not this icy noise grating
at the foundations of my house

>it is the angel's manner of parting
>the waters that drop from
>above and awaken the bodies
>while enclosing the spirits

the shaking earth breaks the air
as I invoke you and your splendid
front because of your entirety
and its creation

>soon respiration will
>consume the air in the room
>and the angel will liberate
>our breathing

III

the angel steps inside
the air leaves the room
it is whiteness made of sun
because bliss has appeared

> from a distant place
> your voice comes conjuring

—Let lips link their spirits—
the angel says and I know
that you live for me and are
regal in stillness golden of skin

> the sounds are the strange
> fragments of a missive long
> ago lost in the tinctures

your lips remain all around
your words as they move inward
of your landscapes and spread
the endless lattice of our days

> —what could restrain me dies out
> of my mind when I stand in your
> presence—the angel says to tell you

IV

the days with and without our fingers
in attendance of our hands my thumb
in your mouth yours in mine as you
honour me from beneath I watch over us
so you may glimpse inside as a third hand
is held detached from me if only for a second

> not to kiss but momentarily to sing
> and praise your face and your hair
> and further because your mind sings and
> turns everything into the complicated
> beauty of these convulsions

WHISPER

V

sometimes your silence is added to the
sound of my voice and I allow reverie
to come in through a door guarded by the
angel—he wills a sweet sleep perhaps
ensuring a new way of dreaming
by spreading his wings wide until
overtaking this space and the objects
in it

       the conundrum may be technical
       and we must seek solace from these
       upturned humours by moving down
       ward of the letters that flow in and
       out of words much as living fire does
       when sound is reversed inward of throat

awake now I close my eyes and recall
Dante's words—I seemed to see a cloud
the colour of fire in my room and in that
cloud was a lordly man frightening to behold
yet apparently marvellously filled with joy

       we'll let fire grow teeth eat
       away at tissues that give form
       to certain organs without skin
       touching skin attenuating
       caressing beginning healing

VI

—spring will soon—says the angel
dawn of new waters like these ones
with both sunrise and sunset made
visible in translucence

> a spectacle this dreaming
> awake is held in your hand
> over my hand our thumbs
> and fingers symmetrically
> placed one on the other

the joining of our dreams has
perhaps begun and we will know when
the offerings are made to those who
are truly young even as the years
pass and we are or are not inside
the deathless who come up
for air because they live inside water

> I promise to watch as you move
> deep inside your dream while you
> speak to me of earth moistened
> with ointments altogether
> unrelated to the aromas of the night

VII

The angel has moved in he breathes
warmly like one of those feral
creatures we take to bed with us

       now your bliss has appeared
       let's not dilate let's press
       your ear to the ground and
       listen to the liquids that
       course inside the earth's cavity

perhaps it is about allowing for a
gathering of our ghosts and it may
be why we frequently converse with
water guttering source of sound
this our constant pulling of speech
toward an imperceptible centre

       the garden is vibrating
       all of a sudden

let us become a single throat that opens

THE O
ELEC

RGASM
GIES

A woman's heart is ever fonder toward an absent lover. Yet no woman retires to bed alone

—Propertius, Elegies: Book II

The Orgasm Elegies

Deepening my habit I think of you. Caught up in circles my labours
cradle your entirety and the present replications of you double triple

you achingly I fall time after time with you here hourly every second
and the clock ticking as you move back and forth lift endless spillikins

never disturb the pile. Vatic are your fingers racing across keys the
sounds are being poured into vessels of coloured glass the heart placed
on your

chest your sex again even if you fall I will catch you and gently place
your body on mine open your mouth pour the sweet honey my own
soft

fluttering. Quieting water: Dominant you my muse become a swan
beads for feathers your skin gold collar as the chain is pulled we turn
time

after time you return to a form made of pearls around neck droplets
liquid skin tightening the noose myself sweet handsome friend I can
       tell you truly

when you come the bindings tighten. I climb above. Draw me to you
so we may rise to that infinity of mirrors kaleidoscopic heavens in your
       eyes

while the multitude of angels stay suspended and the hand of the
Invisible One rouses you through me: there must be an angel playing
       with my heart

containing us shouting out our devotion to Venus Cock-Swallower
       who rises
vast with lands you place before us so the obstacles be set deep within

you. Even. With longing drawing us away elsewhere in you there
       must be
an angel to stop the manifold pain since you must suffer to deserve joy.

Let's set free the fluttering of wings waken the day to a multitude of
        angels
and may they invade your spaces turning them to light as you murmur
        the song

and break free. Dictate you say for you are on top. I know you're
        changeable.
Touch yourself you say in the way you handle your love. It is you
        on top

I say. And I think that as a chevalier you should remain heart-struck for
good. Joy and woe I have in full on my side too. Stay awhile and come

at sunrise when we are confused with the crackling linens. Visit. Set
        yourself as
watchman against my slander but come or not and yes come and be

when the writings are due. If I am to profess that I am to rule from
        above from
under me you can rule and make yourself and ordain the pent-up
        want

mine yours for I can only burn dressed or in my bed. Let divinity wrap
me in you unwrap lightly these fingers open yourself lovely Lover

gracious kind. When will I overcome your fight? If I could lie with you
        Dante once
said also at morning. And D is for dawn rising sun. When I think that
        I'm alone

a feathered hand touches and cleaves my getting to here. Old life
and New life beginning and let's O if I had that knight to caress

would that all the murmurs were of water made. Vita. Your Vita. Mine.
If I had us and we were daily queen and king I would say come let us

delight ourselves with love and repeat the constant invention of day
always make yours the beginning of mine renew the tongue sketch lines

of skin made liquid sourcing at the tip when I hold your eyes in my
hand clutch your voice and I follow you and I still obligate this heart.

The stag is caught fast till an arrow pierces. Yes these are the waters
        that bear
you its waves lapping another shore turning your gaze west where this

body stretches out to reach your magnitude. You born of sea and made
of sand and volcanic matter a continent brought forth daily for my
        creation.

New suns illuminate the surfaces. Violet-dark spring and altar of the
        mighty
Kronos is your origin mine is utterance and they gave me a branch of
        springing

bay. Lordship of love ah my good my coveted lover forge the bodies now
is the time for disciplined toes in mouth gracious pouring coloured
        brightly.

Sand moulds two bodies into one. Before the waters harden let's sway
while color lights up your face let's sway make ready our parts for
        worship

for you seem wondrously filled with joy blessed one who are for ever
and first and last always to sing praises. I do. Dissimilar are your sides

but still you say, hey, poet, you want a theme? Take that! There you are
like any other cupido carefully choosing your arrows to lay me low.

Announce your return already bind your blonde hair tight and let's
alternate taking it and giving it a bit longer hands raised in surrender

little blooms between your legs radiate up and down your thighs
this tongue goes on speaking as I place a wreath of myrtle and yoke up

your mother's pigeons. Opening you up I go. I see the ones left
behind you the besotted youths and maidens who still pine. Up your

back this tongue goes on wanting you to dwell with each other away
from one and the other and hide perhaps inside the tree trunk reside

with the torch burning fiercely and never go out. Always say yes.
Duets sometimes disavowed the little songs we write denied

some of the time and at other times not. I do not divide the words. They
form on lips rounding cock and speak a language uttered of

mouth. Chapter One I think I fell in love with you on and on we write
the song a vigil no longer for if I did not lose my powers and were free

enough to question you your answer would remain the libretto d'amore
you write in quella parte del libro. Always the beginning always writing

inscribing on the heart the words of our desperate state describing
always de la mia memoria yours not always eating the heart while the
          heart

comes to this mouth and I say the second part begins here as I
tremble. A multiplicity of days make up years of joy and loss and sand

between teeth grating and as my fear is most extreme your lovely parts
I conjure eyes closed and assemble you chain two friends together

by means of the sudden appearance of your twin you change your
place in this world bifurcating sexes I get on top. One alternates

with the other vows you make to confuse me overwhelmingly at
one end. I touch myself friend if you had just one fourth of this aching

the waters would part would turn solid altered matter made of glass
would they become. Entering tearing at this spine and stiffening

not arresting against my slander and without my request my left side
curves I touch myself: I want you to love me. Do me. Do to me things.

Do. May the gadgets turn to flesh animate cock yours here between
these hands as I bear down dew of morning mine between legs yours

my fear is most extreme. I begin gathering the little blooms that nestle
at your armpits I find myself making myself from you and out of you

without you even. Always I act pursuant of old themes. Love yours
is mine mine is yours Incipit vita nova daily renewing daily restoring

daily for all time let it be known your parts are mine to have or not
but to excess start the calling daily giving daily adorning daily coming

daily getting to coming daily my sense my life my eyes! Lovely lover
daily and many times daily I bind you to me daily at the ankles the

silk ropes tied to wrists mine for greatly I am tried even as from above
the tightness is felt in throat behind tongue not for any gain to
              endeavour

daily the Dauphin heir apparent of the kingdom coming. Smoke in
your hair between your lips hiding behind your throat and your

tongue speaking your vows to me Amore e 'l cor gentil sono una cosa
always yes between us immediately even if suspended in time straight

away even if delayed by contingencies draw out the days intolerably
importantly probably certainly positively come doubtless and after

having dealt with Love in the last poem invoke your image always
the likeness yours is Love and getting to coming. Let's. Soon.

The veil is drawn away from between us clairvoyance perception
and second sight are invoked by a Sybil who is Oracle because she

speaks somewhere between this and that time held in suspension.
Also stopped space. Arrest time but come do what you can to show

your meaning only as the snakes of sadness tighten the grip around
your tongue mine is uttering signification in screams sometimes
        whispers.

A curbed vow silences the past within. Still you must be brave
thrust ahead do what you can Ingegnati, se puoi, d'esser palese you

make your meanings visible conceal the strata daily though the former
were earlier formed in dream. Let's be. Let's dream. Let's dare to cut

fetters tie them to my song yes I know that. I am adding a stanza
between my legs where they meet your heart. You are the up version

of down because of your ghosts and the rules that govern the dark
inside. For now give me everything I desire love gracious one
        temporary

being without blood to pass as you return from the East to the West
with your mouth cradling the world and its tumult and my attendant

wonder for no one on earth could feel like this I'm thrown and over-
blown with bliss with you here hourly every second sixty times per
          minute

your fingers race across skin and I am reminded that one May morning
on the Malvern Hills a marvel befell me. I was a child then and now

and ashes to ashes funk to funky we know Major Tom's a junkie. Draw
me adorn yourself and may we become the garden inside ourselves

flowers in our mouths your mother's violets. Violet is name of
origin of whom I am repeated forward do what you can to show your

meaning that I may become accustomed again to your signification and
its blood. I wake up by your side and I most carefully invoke these

lines while we go on building temples and together write this sentence
Audite quanto Amor le fece orranza. Comes the summer at its end as

other seasons do when your hand raises the stars from this spine up
higher are held the gems of joined spirit changed to gleaming fires and

still keeping the appearance of a crown it takes its place and we go on
dreaming awake drenched in light. When I place my ear to your throat
        you say

Oh Beatrice let's start in the middle work our way back go forward day
after day let the sounds echo inside us as we come together in radiant
        embrace.

Prayer Star

The ages raise up your laurels to the stars, beloved;
for your light, may you be set apart as auspicious
—Publilius Optatianus Porphyrius

Divinity raises you with you without you shouting this hymn
And crossed by birds is darkness inside where the murmurs are.

Vision of stars in each of your eyes, shift your gaze to me. I am your
Isis, illuminating our night the configuration of stars where

Dismemberment may still be ours together may we reconfigure
Days for the eye that follows you inside this constellation heaven's

Arms enveloped the world once of mud the seasons their dispassion.
Votive lights on sounds moist reverberations and rain to rest at last

Inside the temple prayer spreads sound all around us lifting us. Raise
Day lift us out of night out of complaint put in its place the hymn

Dawns in this throat now joined at tongues when you return us to us.
Amor it is endless this longing, this being of flesh and bone and blood

Vita let's come alive in this place elsewhere soon conjure
Immediately may we be together beyond with strangeness renewing us

Doll we make ourselves as we force us with ourselves in my throat
Despite ourselves denial arrives slowly it repeats itself in your distance

Avidity I swallow our union with my sex worship your
Voice without stopping always seeing you your eyes facing mine

Infinitely there with all manner of plants growing on you from you.
Dominion of rich flora tulips spring crocuses now at your armpits

Dividing petals shooting up this spine pain straightening me I am
Above. Who is under? Who on top? Let us not argue about states for

Vitality is with colours tingling on skin made liquid pouring
Itself into me when in embrace you arrive and begin your

Dance and the words pour out of your mouth black red letters carved
Delirium of utterances transferred constantly. Do not forget I am
        your

Acolyte. In the middle of a field is the bed with you supine I am
Virtuous treading on you carefully disturbing the softness in your

Interior I must gather strength constantly and for the ages for us
Define prayer as meaning in us and into us flows meaning in meaning

Deep in the room is your shrine with my things illuminating. Look
Absorb the outside see the world its kaleidoscopic suspensions

Virtual spaces where you plant your feet if briefly. Be be be be be be be
Into being with me while I go on repeating thrilling I go remaking Isis

Delighting I go constructing your dream making order out of sound
Despite your silence I go on spinning the thread weaving fabrics

As the old waft is done redone the image unfolds vast upon
       surfaces
Vivifying these valuable treasures warmth of blood of gold

Ingots molten and hoarded wealth: emeralds pearls ebony ivory
Dozens more things inside this chest which groans under the weight of

Decembers adding red letter days to anniversaries ponderously
Adding width horizontally spreading over us. May our home be

Verdant beneath floors and walls where grows a garden. Let us not
Isolate this voice from prayer. Prayer star rule over this year of 2015

Dash scarcity of spirit spell away fear keep this voice uttering song
Absorb sounds in mouth and make mouth make tongue intone

Voice. May you be set apart as auspicious beloved on this day
Immanence pervades all: may you be set apart as auspicious

Dearest your light your eyes
           on this day
                may you be set
                     apart as
                        auspicious.

NOTES

The title of the book is inspired by Camper Van Beethoven's *Our Beloved Revolutionary Sweetheart*

The sources used in the book are as follows:

TIED UP

High Priestess
Dedicated to Robin Kay
John Boutté, "Treme Song"

So soon as the front of you
Maximianus, App.1.5–20 Fo, trans. David R. Carlson

Tied Up
Blink 182, "Please Tell Me Why"
Dante, La Vita Nuova (Oxford: Oxford University Press, 1992)
Jaufre Rudel in *Seven Troubadours: The Creators of Modern Verse*,
    by James J. Wilhelm (University Park: The Pennsylvania State
    University Press, 1970)
Russell Smith in *What I Meant to Say: The Private Lives of Me*,
    ed. Ian Brown (Toronto: Thomas Allen Publishers, 2005)

Because I Am Beatrice

Dante Alighieri, *La Vita Nuova* (Milano: Carlo Signorelli Editore, 1968)

Dante Alighieri, *Vita Nuova*. Trans. with introduction by Mark Musa
(Oxford: Oxford University Press, 1992)

Georg Luck, *Arcana Mundi Magic and the Occult in the Greek and Roman Worlds* (Baltimore: The Johns Hopkins University Press, 2006)

THEODORAE BIBLIOTECA

Justinian's Dream

I. His Emergence

Opening theme of "The Rocky and Bullwinkle Show"

Elvis Costello, "Everyday I Write the Book"

Tupac Shakur, "California Love"

II. The Lonely Wilds

Ovid, Metamorphosis Books 1–8. Loeb Classical Library (Cambridge: Harvard University Press, 1977)

III. Everyday He Writes the Book

"Lord Aymar" by Raimbaut de Vaqueiras in www.trobar.org/troubadours/misc/

Elvis Costello, "Everyday I Write the Book"

IV. Kali Cali Throughout

Tupac Shakur: "California Love"

ISIS UP IN THE AIR

Every Door Has Two Fronts

Ovid, *Fasti*. Trans. James G. Frazier. Loeb Classical Library (Cambridge: Harvard University Press, 1996)

Ovid, *Metamorphoses*. Books 1–8. Trans. Frank Justus Miller. Loeb Classical Library (Cambridge: Harvard University Press, 1977)

"Beatritz the Countess of Dia," in *Seven Troubadours: The Creators of Modern Verse*, by James J. Wilhelm (University Park: The Pennsylvania State University Press, 1970)

Guillem IX, Duque of Aquitaine, in *Proensa: An Anthology of Troubadour Poetry*, selected and trans. Paul Blackburn (Berkeley: University of California Press, 1978)

Eros, Too

Ovid, *Metamorphoses* Books 1–8. Trans. Frank Justus Miller. Loeb Classical Library (Cambridge: Harvard University Press, 1977)

César Moro, "Love Letter" (my translation of "Carta de amor")

Elvis Costello, "Everyday I Write the Book"

Hesiod, *Theogony and Works and Days* (Oxford: Oxford University Press, 2008)

The Delightful Love of Bacchus

Nonnos, *Dionysiaca* Books 36–48. Trans. W. H. D. Rouse. Loeb Classical Library (Cambridge: Harvard University Press, 1940)

William Shakespeare, *The Tempest*. (Toronto: The New American Library, 1964)

Ovid, *Metamorphoses* Books 1–8. Trans. Frank Justus Miller. Loeb Classical Library (Cambridge: Harvard University Press, 1977)

A Story of Egypt, Twisted

Written in memory of Gwendolyn MacEwen, upon request from Kitty McKay Lewis for a piece on this great poet for the online weekly publication brickbooks.ca.

Gwendolyn MacEwen, *The T. E. Lawrence Poems.* (Oakville: Mosaic Press/Valley Editions, 1982)

Isis Up in the Air

Ovid, *Fasti.* Trans. James G. Frazier. Loeb Classical Library (Cambridge: Harvard University Press, 1996)

Begins the Bright Season

Anonymous troubadour in www.trobar.org/troubadours/misc/

THE IMPORTANCE OF HUMAN ROMANCE

Dante, *La Vita Nuova* (Oxford: Oxford University Press, 1992)

Various, in *Seven Troubadours: The Creators of Modern Verse,* by James J. Wilhelm (University Park: The Pennsylvania State University Press, 1970)

THE ORGASM ELEGIES

The Orgasm Elegies

Ovid, *Metamorphoses.* Books 1–8. Trans. Frank Justus Miller. Loeb Classical Library (Cambridge: Harvard University Press, 1977)

Cindy Lauper, "Time After time"

Tibors, in Meg Bogin, *The Women Troubadours* (Markham: Penguin Books Canada, 1980)

Eurythmics, "There Must Be an Angel [Playing with My Heart]"

"Beatritz the Countess of Dia," in *Seven Troubadours: The Creators of Modern Verse*, by James J. Wilhelm (University Park: The Pennsylvania State University Press, 1970)

Dante Alighieri, *La Vita Nuova* (Milano: Carlo Signorelli Editore, 1968)

Macabrun in *Seven Troubadours: The Creators of Modern Verse*, by James J. Wilhelm (University Park: The Pennsylvania State University Press, 1970)

Dante Alighieri, *Vita Nuova*. Trans. with an introduction by Mark Musa (Oxford: Oxford University Press, 1992)

David Bowie, "Let's Dance"

Elvis Costello, "Everyday I Write the Book"

The Pretenders, "Talk of the Town"

Divinyls, "I Touch Myself"

David Bowie, "Ashes to Ashes"

William Langland, "The Vision Concerning Piers Plowman"

Beatritz the Countess of Dia, in *Seven Troubadours: The Creators of Modern Verse*, by James J. Wilhelm (University Park: The Pennsylvania State University Press, 1970)

ACKNOWLEDGEMENTS

My gratitude goes to A.F. Moritz for guiding me through the editorial process that gave final form to this book. As with my previous work his advice has proven essential to me. A workshop on the Canadian long poem lead by Jay MillAr provided the key that opened that special space where poetics of wider breadth can be suspended, stretched and contracted as needed. Earlier versions of a few of these poems appeared in *La Chasse à l'objet du désir: Exposition collective internationale*; *What Will Be: Almanach of the International Surrealist Movement*; *Rampike*; *The Annual*; *Juniper: A Poetry Journal*.

Beatriz Hausner has published several poetry collections, including *The Wardrobe Mistress*, *Sew Him Up*, and *Enter the Raccoon*. Her selected poems, poetry collections and chapbooks have been published internationally and translated into several languages. Hausner is a respected historian and translator of Latin American Surrealism, with recent essays published in *The International Encyclopedia of Surrealism* in 2019. Her translations of César Moro, the poets of Mandrágora, as well as essays and fiction by legends like Aldo Pellegrini and Eugenio Granell have exerted an important influence on her work. Hausner's history of advocacy in Canadian literary culture is also well known: she has worked as a literary programmer in Toronto, her hometown, and was Chair of the Public Lending Right Commission. She is currently President of the Literary Translators' Association of Canada, a position she held twice before.

PHOTO: CLIVE S. SEWELL

Colophon

Manufactured as the first edition of
Beloved Revolutionary Sweetheart
in the spring of 2020 by Book*hug Press

Edited for the press by A.F. Moritz
Copy edited by Stuart Ross

Type + design by Gareth Lind / Lind Design
Set in Kievit Serif, designed by Michael Abbink
and Paul van der Laan in 2019, and Xctasy Sans, digitally engineered by
Steve Jackaman, based on the original Willard T. Sniffin design of 1933

bookhugpress.ca